THE MAD® BOOK OF SEX, VIOLENCE AND HOME COOKING

Written by

Dick De Bartolo

Illustrated by

Harry North

Edited by

Nick Meglin

WARNER BOOKS

A Warner Communications Company

WARNER BOOKS EDITION

Warner Books, Inc.
666 Fifth Avenue
New York, N.Y. 10103

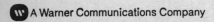 A Warner Communications Company

Printed in the United States of America

First Printing: May, 1983

Reissued: March, 1989

10 9 8 7 6 5 4 3 2

CONTENTS

AN ILLUSTRATED FOREWORD

HOW THIS BOOK CAME TO BE

By
Dick De Bartolo

"I had a theory—that sex and violence was being used to **seduce** Americans and **force** them into spending their hard earned bucks! But was my theory valid? I thought I'd ask my secretary, Ginger Jugs!"

"I pushed my intercom button and asked Ginger to come into my office.

She entered, one long luscious leg after the other..."

"Ginger was tall, stacked! She couldn't type, but she could play the blues on a trumpet in a way that left men weak!"

"This was no **ordinary** secretary! You didn't ask her about **sex** and **violence** without warming up the subject first..."

"Not wanting others to hear, I whispered my question in her ear! My breath was hot and heavy..."

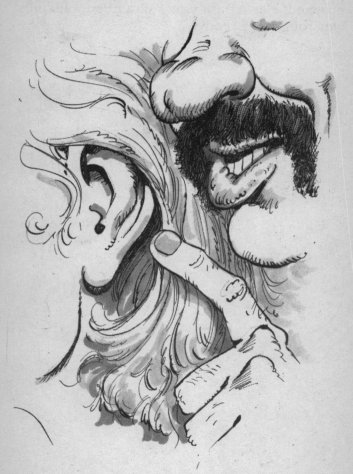

"As she turned to answer, I was intoxicated by her wild and pungent perfume! I was unable to move my head away fast enough—our lips brushed! Her mouth was soft and supple, mine was rough and ready..."

"I was correct! She agreed! Sex **was** definitely being used to seduce people! Movies, television and magazines were full of it! Even rotten **paperback books** were using it as a come on!"

"So I was right about sex, but what about violence? Did people actually **want** to see violence? I had a hunch they did! I decided to talk to the publisher of this book **directly** about my theory! He put off my calls for weeks, so I decided to visit him in person..."

"I was talking, but I don't think he was listening. His mind was drifting. I decided to get his attention, but **good!**

"I spelled out my theories, and I punctuated them in a way he won't soon forget!"

"The creep began to understand that violence is all around us! It's even used to make **business deals**! And speaking of such things, I was given a contract and a cash advance to write a book about **sex** and **violence**!"

"As I turned to leave, the publisher's secretary entered to see what the commotion was! She was beautiful and built! She gave me a knowing wink and motioned toward the sofa! Could it be? In one day was I going to get a book contract and a mid-day romp? This was really the icing on the cake!"

"Then it dawned on me, I couldn't do it! I had to save the "icing on the cake" part for the HOME COOKING section of my book! The secretary's feelings were shattered!"

"She tried playing the blues, but it didn't work... she didn't have a trumpet! And you just can't blow good blues on a typewriter! Better luck next time, sweetheart..."

"And that's how this book came to be! By the time you've finished reading it, you'll know how to avoid being suckered into buying things that pander to your sexual and violent instincts! Consider the money you've already wasted on this trash, the cost of your first lesson!"

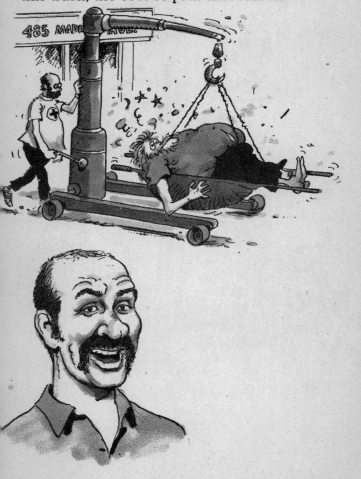

There are certain occupations associated with glamor and sex—television, movies, and the fashion industry, for example. Schools that teach these careers always remind prospective students of this in their TV advertising. And other schools are imitating their successful approach...

MEN—Here's a career that spells MACHO with a capital "M"
The sexy world of the auto mechanic!

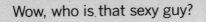

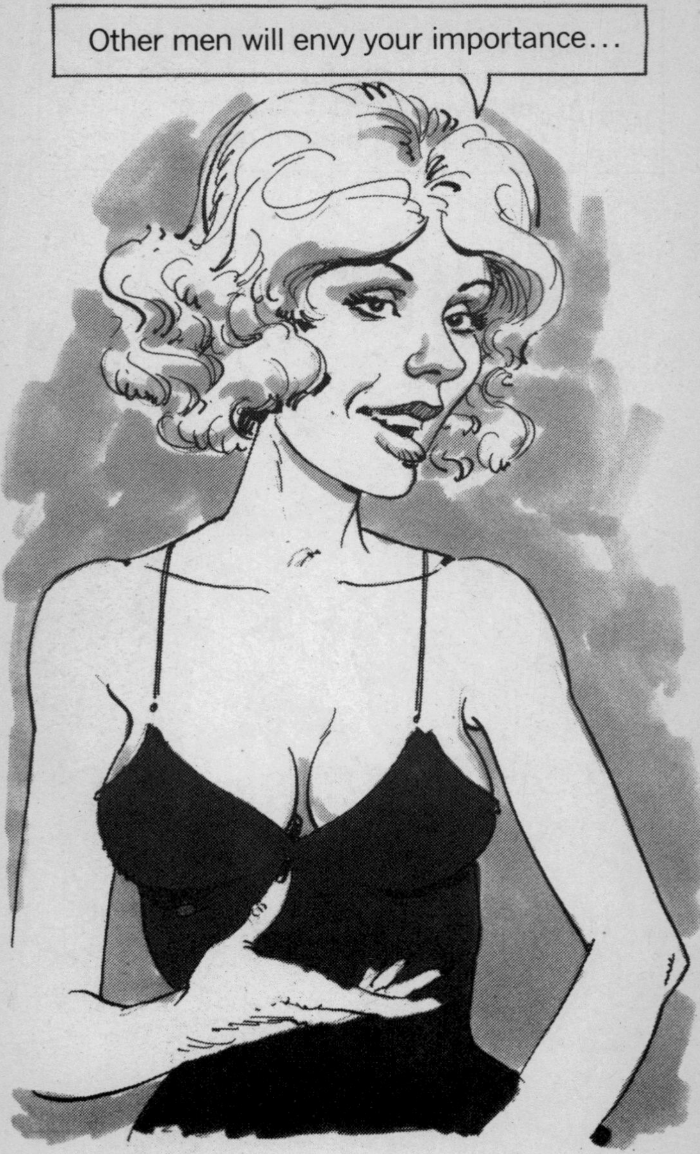
Other men will envy your importance...

...but not only TV advertisers have reached such heights of absurdity—others have discovered the word "designer" has great sexual impact on the buying public! Naturally, they apply it to *anything*, regardless how remote the connection! What? You want *more*? Tell you what we're gonna do! We're gonna give you—free of charge—some examples of

TYPICAL MAGAZINE ADS...

What do sanitation engineers notice most? That's easy...the gal who uses...

From Sassoon St. Lawrence comes the new *Continental Garbage Can Collection!*

Six sexy colors —eggshell white
—lemon-peel yellow
—apple core red
—coffee-grind brown
—mildew green
and tea bag tan

DESIGNER
GARBAGE CANS!

Remember, with a Continental Garbage Can at your doorstep, they may come to pick up your *garbage* during the day, but they'll come back to pick *you* up at night!

EVEN IF YOU'RE STILL GET WITH GOOD DESIGNER

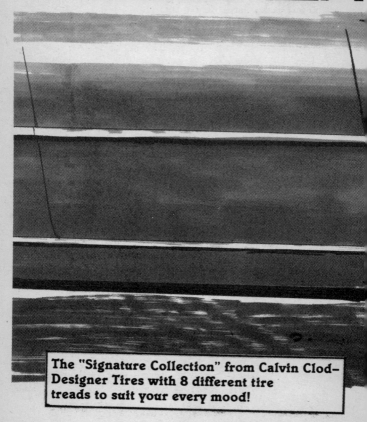

The "Signature Collection" from Calvin Clod—
Designer Tires with 8 different tire
treads to suit your every mood!

FLAT YOU'LL ATTENTION 'N' RICH TIRES

When it comes to military weapons, *might* is important, but isn't *sight* important too? That's why GM introduces

DESIGNER

TANKS

Breath-taking on the battlefield, cute in combat, and dazzling in the ditches, these chic tanks are real *attention getters!* As a matter of fact, they just might take the enemy's minds off the battle long enough for us to chalk up a victory!

Available in *FOUR* popular military colors—*Khaki Brown*
Marine Blue   ***Coast Guard White***   ***Navy Navy***
Now, thanks to GM, more than *soldiers* can be decorated!

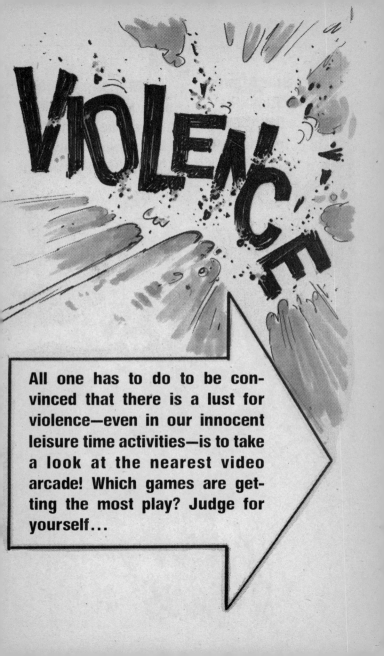

VIOLENCE

All one has to do to be convinced that there is a lust for violence—even in our innocent leisure time activities—is to take a look at the nearest video arcade! Which games are getting the most play? Judge for yourself...

SEX APPEAL

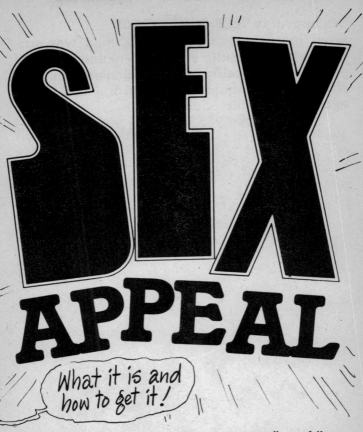

What it is and how to get it!

There is a difference between "sex" and "sex appeal." It's usually easier to find the latter than the former! (Also, you don't run a risk of getting a social disease if you have sex appeal!) What exactly **is** sex appeal? Although the definition defies clinical analysis, the subject can be broken down into component parts...

Sex appeal is SELF CONFIDENCE...
From his primitive beginnings, man was surrounded by a hostile environment and beasts of prey. It was his **self-confidence** that gave him the strength to be quick-witted, strong and brave against incredible odds...

Today, it is that same **self-confidence** that seems to make certain men stand out from the rest when they enter a crowded room...

Sex appeal is BODY LANGUAGE...

Sometimes our bodies can speak louder than our actual voices. If you are keenly aware of those people around you, you can always pick the one who is saying nothing verbally about sex, but through **body language**, is giving off subtle sexual vibrations...

Were you sharp enough to pick out the girl lying on the bar as the one expressing sexual body language? You were? You've got the idea! If you didn't choose her, don't despair—just plan on doing some additional reading. We suggest two other books, "How To Become a Hermit" and "The Celibacy Handbook!"

Sex appeal is VERBAL COMMUNICATION...
It is amazing how many people are afraid to
speak up at a party, a bar, a nightclub, or any
social gathering. Yet, just a few simple words like
"I love that dress," or "you really belong here"
can be the start of a long, rewarding relationship.
(Just a couple of cautions—don't say too much!)

Sex appeal is SENSUOUSNESS...
Sensuousness is that extra "spark," that "glow," that zest for life some people radiate. It is "animal magnetism!" (Sometimes a shower and a deodorant can help!)

Sex appeal is APPEARANCE...

Contrary to popular belief, your sex appeal does not depend on your **looks!** This is **good news** for the guy who doesn't look like Robert Redford, or the girl who doesn't look like Bo Derek! (Of course it's always **better** news for the girl who **does** look like Bo Derek, and the guy who looks like Robert Redford, but it's worse for the girl who looks like Robert Redford and the guy who looks like Bo Derek!) The main thing is good grooming and physical cleanliness. Judge for yourself—here are two guys, one guy is average, has neatly groomed hair and clean clothes. The other guy is rich, is wearing expensive clothes, but lacks personal hygiene. Which guy is a girl mostly like to go for? That's right, the average neatly groomed guy—**every time!***

*This is, of course, a crock! But no **rich** guy needs a book like this, only average guys! So we have to lie a little!

Sex appeal is EMPATHY...
People are drawn to other people who have the
power to understand and feel what someone
else is going through. It is the ability to be
compassionate that adds much to a person's sex
appeal. So, in conversation, empathize with
others. Tell them you understand. However,
don't **overdo** it...

VIO-LENS DEPT.

What did movies like *King Kong*, *Mighty Joe Young*, *Rodan*, *Jaws*, *Jaws II*, *Tarantula*, *Alligator*, *Orca*, *The Thing*, *Alien* have in common? Mainly, they all featured creatures that were less than desirable pets! They wrecked cities, crushed people and, worst of all, had *bad breath!* But none featured a creature so violent so...so...ECCHY as...

DANGER
TOXIC WASTE
RADIOACTIVE
POISONOUS
DEATH-CAUSING
YUUCH!

R-KILOH

ONE MONTH LATER (ACTUALLY ONE *PAGE* LATER!)

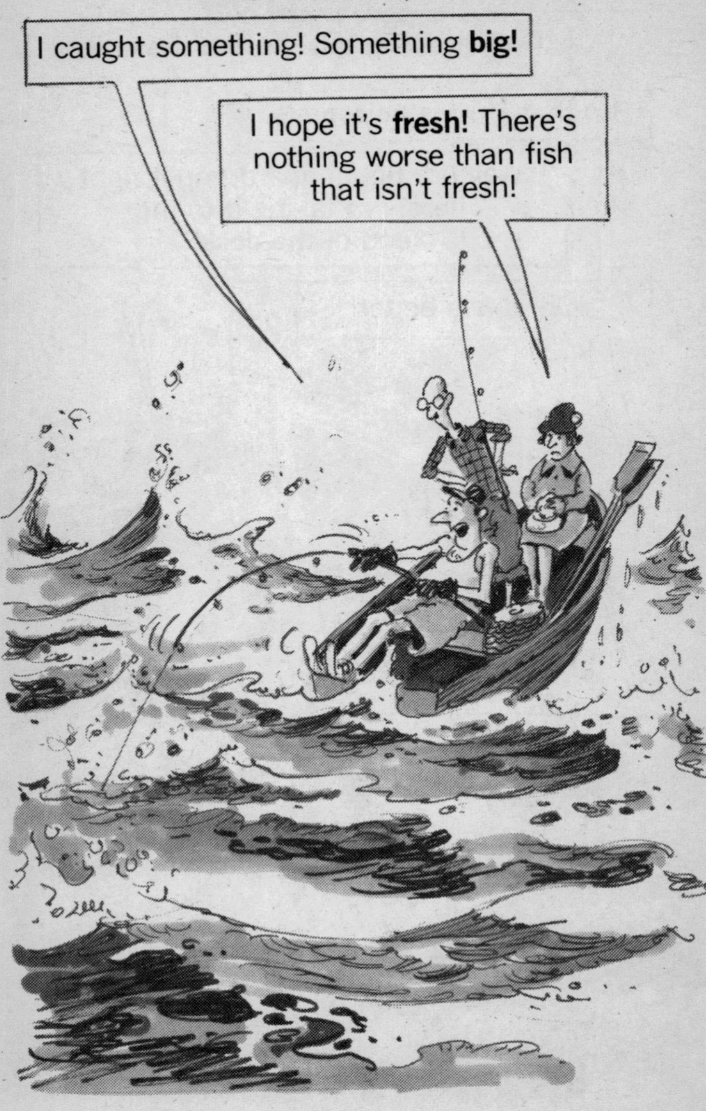

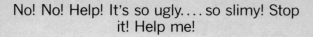

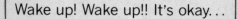

Moments ago another teen-age girl was found roaming the shoreline near the Brooklyn Bridge in hysteria. She claims some big, slimy thing was all over her...
See, nurse— I told you!
That boyfriend of yours **does** get around!

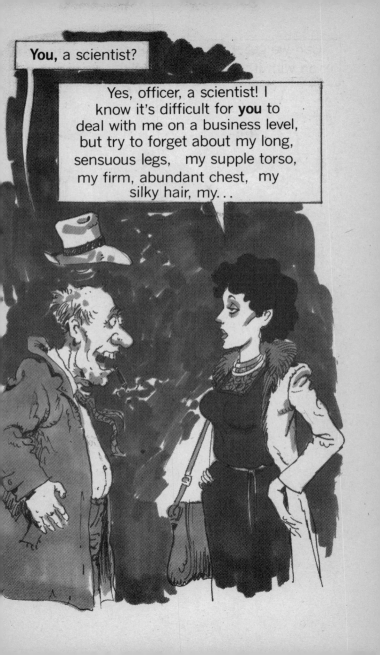

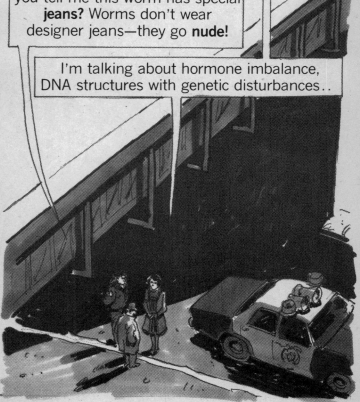

Ladies and gentlemen, I have been informed by the transit authority that the worm took a local train to Boro Park in Brooklyn! On the way there, the worm got covered with 9 coats of **graffiti!** At this moment... **wait!** I've been told that police chief Marvin Turetsky is on the line...

Sure you can learn about sex from seminars and surveys! Sure, Masters and Johnson, The Hite Report, The Playboy Forum, etc. can be very informative about this sensitive subject! But where can you learn about things those famous sources don't dare to deal with? Where else?

The S.V. & H.C. SEX REPORT

*

Initials for **Sex**, **Violence** & **Home Cooking**, dummy!

1. 98% of the men interviewed were unable to function normally when they felt they were being "timed" by their mate.

2. 78% of the men over 90 who were interviewed said they would give anything to be with a younger woman, but they couldn't remember why.

3. 12% of the women interviewed said they just enjoyed love-making and didn't have to be taken out to dinner or bought presents.

4. 100% of the men interviewed said they NEVER met **one** of the 12% mentioned above.

6.81% of the men interviewed said they would rather watch the Superbowl than make love. The other 19% would like to make love DURING the Superbowl.

7. Most men felt they looked sexier in clothes, than without.

Awareness of VIOLENCE is one thing, *avoidance* of VIOLENCE is something else! To *avoid awareness* is something even more else—but to be *aware* of *avoidance* is what this chapter is all about, mainly...

SURE-FIRE VIOLENCE DETERRENTS

It is best not to wear expensive jewelry in high crime areas, but if you feel you must, "customize" the jewelry so that a thief will forget about messing with you...

T-shirts, jackets and hats with printing on them are very popular. By having your own customized lettering done, you can walk in any rough neighborhood and not worry. Here are some suggestions...

You've heard the old expression about "having eyes in the back of your head!" Well, that old expression is still valid today and can be a great ploy against street violence...

If you wear a business suit to work, you are a prime target for street violence, since a mugger will assume you're a professional person making a high salary...

But with just a few accessories, your "business suit" can clear the way for you...

With proper attire, you can easily blend in with your surroundings...

Vary your daily route traveling to and from work. (True, this ploy can be difficult if you live and work in the same building!)

When you come home from a bank carrying cash, don't travel <u>alone</u>! Bring a friend, or your pet. Some pets are better violence deterrents than others, and often make better friends...

Most men keep their wallets in the rear trouser pocket.
A pickpocket knows this. <u>Fool</u> him!

Don't park your car in a dark, secluded area. Park it where you can keep your eye on it...

If you must carry a shoulder bag, make sure that a hood won't be able to rip it off easily...

If someone drops you off by car, don't let them leave until they see you go into your home safely...

Well, at least <u>you're</u> safe!

If you are out driving and someone in another car attempts to force you off the road, don't panic. Keep blowing your horn! This will bring the police...

And while they're giving you a $50 ticket for disturbing the peace, you can figure out if it was worth it protecting the $12 in your pocket!

The most often encountered problem in meeting members of the opposite sex isn't *what to say* as much as what *not* to say! A good "opening" line can become a "closing" line if *too much* is said! The following chapter may serve as a guide to prevent you from...

CONVERSATIONAL OVER-KILL

ENOUGH

TOO MUCH

ENOUGH

TOO MUCH

TOO MUCH

ENOUGH

TOO MUCH

ENOUGH

TOO MUCH

ENOUGH

TOO MUCH

Live—but perhaps
not for too long, it's
America's newest
TV game show…

BLEEDING
for
DOLLARS

137

But there's more! Johnny Oldson, tell the Wunderlins what **else** they won!

From Cheap Skates Inc., a single roller skate with nylon wheels and defective stainless steel axles! Just place this roller skate on any stairway where the light is dim and wait for the **hilarious** results!

From Rankco, the new **Fry-Baby Kit!** It converts any chair to an **electric chair!** It's wild, it's zany, it's easy, and best of all, it's fun!

Okay, folks! Here's how we're going to play game number two! Before the program, we asked the Whorralls to pick **six gifts** they would really love to win! Now as you can see, we have put those six gifts on the opposite side of the stage...

You see we've given **ten members** of our studio audience **rifles,** and **their** job is to see that you **don't** get those prizes to this side of the stage! We're not only violent on this program, we're also cute!

From Castrato Convertables—a sofa bed with a **big difference!** Sometime during the night, when your overnight guests least expect it, your Castrato Convertable slams shut with a force of **6,000 pounds!**

From PIC-NIC-SICK Plastic comes picnic knives, the special "zany" knives that have **handles** sharper than the **blades!** Turns any picnic into a real "cut up" affair!

So until next week, this is Glen Scartissue saying goodbye to you folks at home! And to you folks in the **audience**—I have a special surprise! There's a **bomb** under one of your seats! Have a **blast!**

Where do people turn when they have questions about sex? Many of them turn to advice columns in their local newspaper! Yes, if you're looking for answers to sex questions, the newspapers are full of it! But we're even more full of it with our very own advice column...

DEAR S.V.H.C.

Dear S.V.H.C.
My boyfriend wants to make love in the
backseat of his car, but I think that's
filthy? What do you think?
                    PROPER GIRL

Dear S.V.H.C.
I think about sex almost all the time. In any given 24 hour period, I think about sex twenty-three hours and my school work for an hour. Is this normal for a teen-ager?

CONCERNED

DEAR CONCERNED:
NO, IT IS NOT NORMAL. WHY DO YOU WASTE AN
ENTIRE HOUR THINKING ABOUT SCHOOL WORK?
WHAT ARE YOU STUDYING TO BE, A GENIUS OR
SOMETHING?

Dear S.V.H.C.
Is it possible to love two men at the
same time?
                    TORN

DEAR TORN:
YES, BUT YOU HAVE TO BE REAL GOOD AT GYMNASTICS!

Dear S.V.H.C.
My girlfriend has given me an ultima-
tum--it's either me or my St. Bernard.
Any suggestions?

PET LOVER

DEAR PET LOVER:
WHY NOT LET YOUR GIRLFRIEND DATE YOU FOR
ONE MONTH AND THEN DATE YOUR ST. BER-
NARD. THEN LET HER MAKE THE FINAL DECI-
SION!

Dear S.V.H.C.
This may sound strange, but I'm looking for a relationship that <u>doesn't</u> include sex. Is there such a thing?

WORN OUT

Dear S.V.H.C.
My boyfriend wants to take my picture nude. Should I let him?

SHY

DEAR SHY:
WHY NOT? HE'LL PROBABLY CATCH A BAD
COLD, BUT THAT'S HIS PROBLEM.

Dear S.V.H.C.
My boyfriend lies and cheats and never does anything he says he's going to do. I think we should break up because I don't think he has any future. What do you think?

FRUSTRATED

DEAR FRUSTRATED:
ARE YOU KIDDING? THIS GUY IS GOING TO
MAKE IT <u>BIG</u> IN POLITICS! MARRY THE BUM
TODAY!

Dear S.V.H.C.
I know this is personal, but what's the furthest I should go with my teenage girlfriend?

EVEN MORE CONCERNED

Dear S.V.H.C.
I come from a very rich family, and I have lots of money myself. I'm afraid boys date me for this reason. How can I tell if a guy is interested in me, or my money?

VERY RICH

DEAR RICH:
SEND US $5000 AND WE'LL TELL YOU HOW YOU
CAN SPOT PHONIES!

Is there really violence in

HOME COOKING?

Of course there is! If there wasn't, would we devote a whole chapter to the subject? Not us! Never happen! Therefore, there **must** be violence in **HOME COOKING**! What's that? You want proof? Okay, sucker—you asked for it...

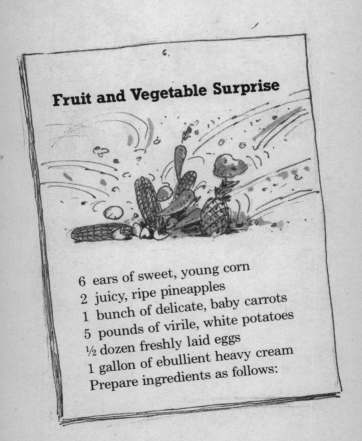

Fruit and Vegetable Surprise

6 ears of sweet, young corn
2 juicy, ripe pineapples
1 bunch of delicate, baby carrots
5 pounds of virile, white potatoes
½ dozen freshly laid eggs
1 gallon of ebullient heavy cream
Prepare ingredients as follows:

Beat eggs

Mash potatoes

Slice carrots

Crush pineapple

And finally, smother everything with violently whipped cream...